Narrowboat Blues

A canal boat comedy drama in one act

Further recent titles from LinguaBooks

Panto
Puss in Boots
Aladdin

Fantasy
The Legend of Sidora

Fiction
The Taste of Rain
A Parting Shot

Language
Gateway English

More information from www.linguabooks.com

Narrowboat Blues

A canal boat comedy drama in one act

by Maurice Claypole

LinguaBooks

Maurice Claypole has asserted his right under the Copyright, Designs and Patents Act, 1988 to be identified as the author of this work.

ISBN (paperback edition): 978-1911369790
eISBN (digital edition): 978-1911369783

First edition

Editor: Ann Claypole

Copyright © 2021 LinguaBooks

All rights reserved. No part of this publication may be reproduced, stored in a retrieval system or transmitted, in any form or by any means, electronic, mechanical, photocopying, recording or otherwise, without the prior permission of the publishers.

A CIP catalogue record for this book is available from the British Library.

This book is sold subject to the condition that it shall not, by way of trade or otherwise, be lent, resold, hired out or otherwise circulated without the publisher's prior consent in any form of binding or cover other than that in which it is published and without a similar condition including this condition being imposed on the subsequent purchaser.

LinguaBooks
Elsie Whiteley Innovation Centre
Hopwood Lane
Halifax HX1 5ER

www.linguabooks.com

Performance Rights

No performances of this work are permitted without the author's express permission.

Production and license enquiries should be addressed to:

LinguaBooks
Elsie Whiteley Innovation Centre
Hopwood Lane, Halifax HX1 5ER
United Kingdom
Tel. 01422 399 554
info@linguabooks.com

Billing and credit requirements

All advertising and publicity material (leaflets, programmes, flyers, posters, etc., including any announcement made via digital or social media) relating to any actual or indented production of this work must include the following billing details, each item of which shall be displayed in a prominent form and position:

Narrowboat Blues
a canal boat comedy drama in one act
by Maurice Claypole
in association with LinguaBooks

About the play

Tom and Bunty are spending their retirement on a canal boat, but things are not as rosy as they seem when their daughter Abby makes a surprise trip home from Spain.

Things are not as rosy as they seem for Abby either. Thankfully, modern technology is on hand to make life easier, until it doesn't, and the local boat electrician is also on hand to help... sort of...

A caring, funny, sometimes melancholic look at narrowboat life with implications that go far beyond the immediate setting.

Table of Contents

First Performance 8
Casting and characters 9
Setting 9
Narrowboat Blues 10
Appendix 1   Music 34
Appendix 2   Set design 37
Appendix 3   Properties list 38
Appendix 4   Sound effects 40

First Performance

First produced by the Halifax Thespians as a socially distanced production filmed at the Halifax Playhouse in June 2021 with the following cast (in order of appearance):

Bunty	Julie Anne Johnston
Chas	Luke Lortie
Tom	Leighton Hirst
Abby	Francesca Foster
Voice of Alexa	Melanie Murray

Directed by	Nigel Town
Assistant director	Sharon Old
Set design	Leighton Hirst
Lighting	Gerard Marescaux
Costumes	Norma Bateman
Props	Janet Clegg

Casting and characters

<u>Casting:</u>

2 M, 2/3 F

<u>Characters</u>

Tom	retired civil servant and volunteer lockkeeper, now trying his hand at writing
Bunty	(nicknamed Bunny) Tom's wife, retired hairdresser
Abby	their daughter
Chas	boat engineer and would-be songwriter
Alexa	a computer-generated voice (pre-recorded or offstage)

Setting

The action of the play is set on the Rochdale Canal in Calderdale, West Yorkshire, and this is reflected in the locations referred to during the play.

If appropriate (for example, to add local colour if performed in the vicinity of a different canal), place names can be changed to reflect a location more familiar to the audience.

Narrowboat Blues

The action takes place inside a narrowboat. The general impression is of a small but cosy lounge with a bunk/settee, coffee table, a small solid fuel stove and a fridge or compact kitchen unit. The desired effect can be achieved with a few simple items of furniture. See Appendix 2 for additional notes on set design.

Entrance stage right is via a short set of steps leading up to the deck (offstage). Exit stage left leads to the bathroom and bedroom.

When entering from stage right, the cast stoop slightly to pass through a (real or imagined) door but return to full height at the bottom of the steps.

On the table are a laptop and a Bluetooth speaker.

Scene 1

Bunty is speaking into her mobile.

Bunty Hello, Abby, dear. How are you? It's been a while. … No, we haven't received a parcel from Amazon. When did you send it? … Oh, well, it should get there in a few days … What? … What do you mean, where am I? I'm at home. … Oh, well, I was at the doctor's this morning and I switch my phone off in the surgery. It interferes with the equipment on cloud nine or something. … *(kettle whistles)* Hang on a minute, the kettle's boiling. *(takes kettle off)* So how's Emilio? … Oh, I'm sorry to hear that. Well, I'm sure you'll get it sorted out soon. What? … I'm

Narrowboat Blues

at home, dear, like I said. ... What? ... You're where? Oh, dear...

Chas *(offstage)* Hello, anybody home? *(enters but remains standing at top of steps, i.e. on foredeck, stoops to peep into lounge).* Hi, Bunty. It's only me.

Bunty *(to Chas)* Yes, what is it? *(to phone)* Look, there's someone at the door. I'll call you back.

Chas Your water tank is full. It was coming out of the overflow, so I've turned the tap off for you. Do you want me to take the hose off?

Bunty Thank you, Chas. That's very kind. *(produces a bottle of Aquasol)* And can you put some of this in, please. A couple of capfuls will do. Then I know the water is fit to drink. Maybe we don't really need it, but it gives me peace of mind. And Tom's had a touchy tummy ever since his op, so it's best to be safe.

Exit Chas with bottle. Bunty fusses making tea, then sits, picks up phone and dials.

Bunty Hello, dear. Now, tell me again – exactly where are you? ... Ah! Well, it certainly is a surprise, dear. We don't live there any more. ... Yes, I know. ... but we had to downsize, you see, after your father took early retirement. ... We didn't want to worry you, but there's no point in beating it out of the bush if you're already here. We've reduced our tangibles and desized our assets ... Yes, what else would I mean? I've said it plainly enough. We sold the house and moved to somewhere more... more bijou. ... Well, you know your father used to be a volunteer lockkeeper... so now we live on the canal ... no, not exactly the lockkeeper's cottage. We live on a narrowboat... but it's very nice. We've got all the odd coms, hot and cold water, cooker, fridge, a nice bathroom. We've got a nice warm stove <u>and</u> central heating. And we have a lovely view of the… er… of the canal. … What? No, I didn't tell you, dear, because we haven't seen you since you moved to Catalante or wherever you are. … Yes dear, we always get cards and parcels because we still use the same address. We have an arrangement with the new owners. We call in from time to time and pick up our post. … Oh, you've met them, have you? Yes, I bet that was a bit of shock. … For them, I mean. … What? Well, I can't leave you stood standing there… I'll come and pick you up. And you can help me with the shopping; I could do with a hand. See you soon.

Ends call, gets coat, shopping bag and exits.

Scene 2

Tom enters from stage left (i.e. from the direction of the bedroom), sits, opens laptop.

Tom   Enable voice, enable dictation, open last document.

(waits briefly between instructions/passages, but gradually speeds up)

History of the Inland Waterways.

New Chapter.

Since the Rochdale canal was re-opened in 2002, it has become a major attraction for leisure boaters and home to a growing community of live-aboards, not to mention fair-weather boaters who spend weekends on the water whenever the weather suits their temperament. One of the joys of boat life is that you can cast off and er… *(searching for words)* ...change the scenery any time you like... *(looks out of the window)* ...but I don't think we'll be going anywhere today. Still looks a bit muggy from all that flooding.

Oh, no. Don't write that, you idiot machine!

Nor that!

Don't you know the difference between dictation and shouting?

Obviously not! *(slams laptop shut in anger)*

(to loudspeaker)

Siri, what's the weather going to be like?

(silence)

Cortana, give me a weather forecast.

(silence)

Oh, god. How am I supposed to remember which one of those women lives in that box?

Alexa, is it you? Are you bloody listening to me?

Alexa Sorry, I didn't understand that. Would you like a list of questions you can ask me?

Tom No, I don't want a bloody list. I want the weather forecast.

(silence)

Alexa, give me a bloody weather report.

Alexa In the British Isles, the weather will be variable with some sunshine, a chance of precipitation and winds varying in strength from a light breeze to heavy gales. Here is the national outlook for the next 24 hours...

Narrowboat Blues

Tom I don't want a national outlook, Alexa. I want to know if it's going to rain here!

Alexa Sorry, but I cannot identify your location.

Tom Why can't you identify my location?

(silence)

Alexa, why can't you identify my location?

Alexa Because you are on a boat.

Tom Are you kidding me?

(silence)

Alexa, are you taking the piss?

Alexa I'm sorry, I don't understand you. Would you like to search the web for 'taking the piss'?

Tom Alexa, why can't you identify my location?

Alexa According to the information available from your previous queries, you are on a narrowboat. The boat is made of steel and is blocking geolocation services.

Tom I'll block your bloody geolocation service in a minute!

(opens laptop)

Got a bit bogged down with the Rochdale – well, you would, wouldn't you? Especially the state the towpath's in at the moment. Let's see where I got to with the Bridgewater... *(dictates)* When the Duke of Bridgewater opened the first modern canal in 1761, this new form of transport halved the price of coal overnight and ushered in the golden age of canal transport. Bridgewater's canal boats were known as 'starvationers' because they were built with protruding frames that looked like the ribs of a starving man. Bugger, that reminds me... *(goes to galley, starts looking in fridge)*. Thought she was going to go shopping. *(smells milk)* And the fridge is off again. Got to get the shore power hooked up properly or it'll be sour milk all week and fish poisoning on Fridays. And warm beer – correction, no beer. *(in desperation)* If you want something brewing, brew it yourself.

Exit stage right.

Scene 3

Enter Bunty and Abby (with luggage and shopping. Items they unpack include toilet rolls and a big pack of men's incontinence pads (Tena Men, MoliCare or similar).

Bunty   Welcome aboard dear.

Abby   *(looking around)* This is nice ... but you can stand up! I always thought you had to stoop down once you got inside.

Bunty   Yes, I know. That's why your dad named it 'Tom's Tardis'...

   (pause as Bunty waits for the penny to drop)

   ...because it's...

Abby/Bunty *(together, laughing)* ...bigger on the inside!

Abby   So how long have you been living on a barge, Mum?

Bunty   Don't call it a barge, dear. You'll upset your father. You don't want him to fire off his candle. A barge is a working boat. And it's wider. This is a narrowboat.

Abby   So... how long?

Narrowboat Blues

Bunty Fifty-five feet, dear. Fifty-seven and a half is the max if you want to go past Sowerby Bridge onto the Calder & Hebble.

Abby I mean, how long have you been living aboard?

Bunty Ah well, you remember that time when your father was ill?

Abby You said he had an infection.

Bunty It wasn't an infection, dear. He just didn't want people to worry.

Abby So what was it? And what's that got to do with living on a boat?

Bunty Well, the waiting list for radiation was so long that we had to have it done privately. Abroad. And that sort of ate up our savings – and in the end we had to sell up and move anyway, and your dad's always fancied owning a boat.

Abby Mum, what are you saying?

Bunty Your dad had a blood test and his PSA was through the roof.

Abby PSA?

Bunty Oh, dear… well, now I've let the rabbit out of the sack, I suppose you ought to know. It stands for prostate something antisomething.

Bunty starts unpacking the shopping.

Abby Oh, my god… but… but… he's cured, right?

Pause.

Narrowboat Blues

Bunty   He's on six-monthly check-ups. After the op, we found they hadn't got it all out. The specialist said we had three cards to play: operation, radiation and hormone therapy.

Abby   What about chemo?

Bunty   That's not much good for what your dad's got, dear.

Abby   But the treatment worked? I mean, he's OK now?

Bunty   We are on our third card – he's on hormones. They keep the testosterone down. So you might find him a bit … different. He has mood swings and stuff. But it's better than the old days. With your granddad, they just chopped off his…. Sh! Your father's coming.

Abby   Oh my god! I must look a mess. Where's the…

Bunty   …bathroom? Just through there, dear. You can't miss it. If you need the you-know-what, just press the big red button to flush it.

Exit Abby stage left.

Enter Tom with beer: a supermarket bulk pack, maybe two. Bunty rushes to help him down the stairs and takes the beer. They engage in a banter routine that they have obviously played out many times before.

Tom   *(cheerily)* Hello, Bunny; it's your honey.

Bunty   Come in dear. Make my day sunny.

Tom   Went to the shop and guess what's funny?

Bunty   I bet you spent all the money.

Tom   Yep. No money for runny honey, Bunny.

   (pause)

Narrowboat Blues

        So I just got beer.

Bunty Give that here. You know you shouldn't lift.

Tom Because I can't hold my water, is that what you mean?

Bunty You know what the doctor said.

Tom I know… I see you got some more of those things. *(indicating box of pads)*

Bunty Well, it's better to be safe than soggy.

Tom We're a right pair, aren't we, Bunny?

Bunty I know… You can drink, but you can't keep it in; I can keep it in, but I'm not supposed to drink. *(mimicking M. Alfonse from 'Allo 'Allo)* It ees my dicky ticker.

Tom *(laughs)* Just keep taking the tablets…

Optional: sound of vacuum flush toilet.
Enter Abby from direction of bathroom stage left.

Abby Hello, Dad.

Pause. Tom looks from one to the other.

Tom What's going on?

Bunty Abby's come to visit. Aren't you pleased?

Tom *(collects himself)* Yes, yes, of course – let me look you.

Abby *(holds out her arms)* Good to see you, Dad.

Tom goes up to Abby, takes her hands, looks her up and down.

Tom You look…

Abby …older?

Narrowboat Blues

Tom   I was going to say… I don't know what I was going to say.

Abby   How about a hug?

They hug, briefly. Tom pulls away.

Tom   So… a celebration. *(pulls out three cans of beer)* I'm afraid we're out of champagne.

Abby   That's fine, Dad.

Tom   I supposed you're more used to Sangria, eh?

Abby   We have beer in Spain, too, Dad.

Tom   Beer is universal proof that someone up there loves us and wants us to be happy.

Bunty   Not for me, I'm afraid. I'll put the kettle on.

Abby   Well, I don't mind if I do.

Tom and Abby open their cans, clink them together and drink. Bunty makes tea.

Abby   Happy days.

Tom   So… er…

Abby   …what brings me here?

Tom   Well, we didn't know you were coming.

Abby   I know. I'm sorry about that.

They sit.

         I just wanted to see you on your birthday.

Tom   My birthday isn't till next week.

Pause.

Narrowboat Blues

Abby   So… I came early… anyway, I get a bit muddled with dates. Sorry.

Tom   Is that why we haven't heard from you for ages?

Abby   Well, it's been a difficult time.

Tom   It's been seven years, that's what it's been. Seven years since you ran off with Francisco from the disco.

Abby   His name's Emilio, and he worked in a tapas bar. Anyway, that was before we settled in Alicante. Or at least, I thought we were settled.

Tom   Well, you never even invited us the wedding. And what now? You caught him with a floozie in the jacuzzi?

Abby   Nothing like that, Dad!

(pause)

Well, actually, yes… something like that.

Bunty   That Emilio. His mother should have thrown him away and kept the stork. I see you've brought some luggage.

Abby   The rest is being sent on.

Tom   Alexa, what is my daughter trying to tell me?

Alexa   I'm sorry. I don't understand.

Tom   Neither do I.

Blackout.

Scene 4

The following week. Evening. Bunty, Tom, Abby and Chas are all sitting in the lounge; wine and beer on the table, candles, festive atmosphere, cake. Chas on guitar. Bunty, Abby and Chas sing Happy Birthday to Tom. Tom blows out candle(s).

Abby   Happy birthday, Dad.

Bunty   Happy birthday, Tom.

Tom   Thank you, honey.

Bunty   May your day be sunny…

Tom   …my jokes funny…

Bunty   …and your pockets…

Tom   …full of money…

Tom/Bunty …to buy runny honey!

Abby   *(to Chas)* They do this all the time.

Chas   Happy birthday, Tom. I brought you something.

Chas hands over a package, which Tom proceeds to unpack, revealing a windlass.

Tom   Thank you, Chas. A windlass… that's very thoughtful.

Chas   Well, I guessed you could use a new one.

Tom   It's Bunty who operates the locks nowadays, but you're right, we lost ours.

Bunty   You dropped it in Black Pit Lock, you mean. *(to Abby)* He let go when he was lowering the gate paddle and it flew right off the spindle. Could have been nasty.

Narrowboat Blues

	(to Chas) That's very kind of you, Chas, but you shouldn't have gone to the trouble.
Chas	No trouble at all; It's a spare that I had anyway.
Tom	Say Chas, when you've got time, do you think you could give me hand with my bow thruster? Seems to be playing up.
Chas	Sure. As soon as I get back from Todmorden. Got a wiring job on there next week.
Abby	Bow thruster? You make it sound like a spaceship, Dad.
Tom	It's the other way around! They try to make Sci Fi spaceships sound like boats, what with all that 'Captain Kirk to the bridge' stuff.
Abby	Oh, dear. I'm never going to get the hang of all this jargon on board. I can never remember which is port and which is starboard.
Bunty	*(to Abby)* Don't be silly, dear. We don't bother with all that nonsense on a narrowboat. We just say left and right. And we don't have 'heads' and 'bunks'; we have a bathroom and bedrooms. Everything's pretty normal really.
Abby	*(starting to tidy up)* Where shall I put this?
Bunty	In the galley. *(pause)* I'll do it. Tom, can you help me clear up?

Bunty and Tom get busy tidying/washing up, leaving Abby and Chas to themselves.
Chas strums a few chords or improvises a brief solo.

Abby	So do you live on board, too, Chas?
Chas	Yes, my dad was a boat outfitter, so I sort of grew up on the cut.

Narrowboat Blues

Abby On the what?

Chas The canal. We say 'cut' because the navvies cut the first canals out of the earth with picks and shovels.

Abby I thought the navvies built the railways.

Chas They built the canals first. That's why they were called navvies – short for navigators, you see. They went wherever the work was. And it was the railways that put an end to freight transport on the canals. Now it's all leisure boaters and live-aboards. But I'm what you call a continuous cruiser.

Abby Bohemian lifestyle, eh?

Chas Well, some people who live aboard, like your mum and dad for instance, have a permanent mooring, but I can't afford one, so I have a continuous cruising license, which means I can't stay in one area for more than two weeks.

Abby But don't you have to go to work?

Chas Like father, like son: Sparky Chas, boat electrician and marine engineer at your service.

Abby And where did you learn to play the guitar?

Chas Oh, I never learned. I just mess around. Helps while away the time, especially when I'm moored in the middle of nowhere. I write stuff, too. Want to hear one of my songs?

Abby I'd love to.

Chas launches into Narrowboat Blues. The song starts rather maudlin, then becomes more upbeat. Optionally Chas may improvise lyrics, replacing 'old canal' and 'lonesome' with local place names. Abby joins in.

Chas I got the blues. I got the blues
I got the lonesome narrowboat blues (2x)

Narrowboat Blues

> I moved on board when I lost my gal
> Now I put my faith in the ... old canal / ... in the *[local name]* canal
>
> I got the blues. I got the blues
> I got the ... *[local name]* ... narrowboat blues
>
> Time is passing by and I'm losing my hair
> People come and go, but the cut don't care
>
> I got the blues. I got the blues
> I got the *[local name]* narrowboat blues
> *(pause)*
> I'm afraid it's not quite finished.

Abby *(applauds)* This is fun – but I guess canal life can be lonesome ... if you live on your own...

Chas In my case, it's just me and Lucy.

Abby Oh! Lucy?

Chas Light of my life.

Pause.

> Lucy's a border collie. You'll like her. She's very affectionate. And she loves living aboard. Well, it's all she's ever known, really. She even puts up with my singing. Do you want to come and meet her?'

Abby Sounds delightful. *(calling across to Bunty and Tom)* I'm just off to have a look at Chas's barge.

Exit Abby and Chas.

Tom It's not a barge!

Blackout.

Scene 5

Several days later. Tom and Chas are stretched out on the floor, Chas's head and torso obscured by the steps. On the floor is a laundry basket. The sound of a hammer tapping against steel can be heard.

Tom   Very kind of you to help out like this, Chas… *(hammer sound becomes louder)* Hang on, you don't need to hit it with a bloody hammer!

Chas   How else do you expect me to shift it? It's all seized up. The motor's virtually welded to the housing.

Tom   That's the trouble with people today… as much patience as a lobster in a pot… doesn't work, bash it with a hammer!

Chas   *(emerging)* Look, I'm only trying to help.

Tom   Oh, I know your sort. First you come sniffing round my daughter, then you try to scupper my boat.

Chas   What did you say?

Tom   You should listen more. Attention span of a dead gnat, some people!

Chas   I've had enough of this. *(storms off)*

Tom   Bugger off and good riddance!

Enter Bunty.

Tom   Hello, Bunny. Did you get my prescription?

Bunty   No, Abby's picking it up on the way back from the solicitor's.

Tom   Well, I need it! Like now! I'm getting no rest and I've got to get on with my book.

Narrowboat Blues

Bunty A man's gotta do what a man's gotta do – and a woman's got to do everything else.

Bunty picks up laundry basket and exits stage left. Tom opens laptop and begins to dictate.

Tom As we have seen, the British inland waterways have undergone many changes throughout their 300-year history and have successfully transitioned from commercial carrying to the leisure industry.

Enter Abby.

Tom *(looking up)* Hello, love. Did you get my prescription?

Abby No, they haven't got it yet.

Tom *(in exasperation)* What the hell is the world coming to? I need one simple thing and I'm surrounded by idiots!

Abby Dad, where's… ?

Tom *(irritably)* Not now. Can't you see I'm working. I've nearly finished the book. Just need a final sentence or two to round it off. And I've got a headache. And the bloody heating's gone off. And your mum's been out all day and I've had sod all to eat. And I need to concentrate.

Abby Have you seen Chas? His boat's not there.

Tom Gone. Smashed my bow thruster and sodded off.

Abby Dad, what have you done? You're getting worse every day.

Tom Well, you can bugger off, too, if you don't like it here. Nobody asked you to come back. Should have stayed in Alicante with your Catalan Casanova, oh, but no, he threw you out, didn't he?

Abby   He did not! I left because he was a selfish pillock like you. He wouldn't settle down. I wanted…

Tom   I don't give a toss what you wanted. I want to be left in peace! And I want to get this thing finished before…

Abby   Did Chas say where he was headed?

Tom   Ain't got much choice, has he? You can only go one way or t'other. Can't stay in one place, anyway, that one, the gormless vagabond. About as much use as a one-legged man at an arse-kicking party.

Abby   Dad, you're impossible!

Abby storms off. Tom turns back to his dictation.

Tom   In 2018, the Canal & River Trust rebranded itself as a wellbeing organisation, focusing more on towpath and canalside activities than on boaters and boating. Whether this will ultimately lead to a change in the nature of our canals, only time will tell. In the meantime, the still waters themselves attest to the folly of mankind's transient pursuit of health, wealth and happiness.

Blackout.

Narrowboat Blues

Scene 6

Two months later. Enter Bunty and Abby in mourning. Bunty is carrying a framed funeral portrait of Tom, which she places in full view.

Abby The vicar was very nice.

Bunty Yes… very nice.

Abby It was a lovely service.

Bunty Yes… lovely.

Abby And I thought Uncle Malcolm did a good job organising the reception.

Bunty Yes… a good job.

Abby Sit yourself down, Mum. I'll make us a cup of tea.

Bunty I've got tea coming out of my eyeballs. Have we got anything stronger? I need something to settle my stomach.

Abby I'll have a look.

Abby fetches a bottle of brandy and two glasses, pours.

Abby Will this do? I'm not sure if it's right for the occasion.

Bunty If not now, then when? It's been in the cupboard a long time.

Abby Well, we gave Dad a good send off, didn't we? Can't do more than that. Cheers.

Bunty Here's to Tom.

Abby To Dad.

They raise a toast.

Narrowboat Blues

Abby   I wish Chas could have been there. He got on all right with Dad until…

Bunty   I know, dear, but we weren't all that close, anyway. He was just a neighbour, and not even that most of the time; always on the move.

Abby   Mum…

Bunty   Yes, dear?

Abby   About Chas…you know I spent some time with him on his boat…

Bunty   Yes, dear, you were helping him bathe the dog or something.

Abby   It wasn't just that, Mum. You see…

Bunty   Not now, dear. It's been a long day and I'm very tired. I think I'll go and have a lie down.

Bunty exits slowly to bedroom.

Abby   Alexa, call Chas.

Alexa   Trying to connect to Chas… I'm sorry. The number you have called is not available.

Abby   Alexa, give me an update on the Rochdale Canal closures.

Alexa   There are currently no navigation closures on the Rochdale Canal.

Abby   Alexa, which boats are currently on the Rochdale Canal?

Alexa   I'm afraid I don't have that information. Please be more specific.

Abby   Alexa, where the hell is Narrowboat Sparky?

Narrowboat Blues

Alexa There is one recent news item concerning a narrowboat called Sparky. Would you like me to read it to you?

Abby Yes!

Alexa Headline: Death on the Rochdale Canal. Text: One death is reported as a narrowboat sank in Punchbowl Lock near the summit. The rear end of narrowboat Sparky was caught on the cill as the lock was emptying. This caused the front end of the boat to fill with water and led to the boat sinking in a matter of minutes…

Abby No! *(swipes the speaker off the table, silencing it, runs offstage into bedroom)*

Mum! Mum! Did you hear that?... Mum! Mum! Wake up! Oh, my god!

Re-enter Abby in panic.

Alexa, call emergency!

Blackout.

Scene 7

A few weeks later. Abby is on her mobile, assuming the same pose as Bunty in Scene 1. Next to Tom's portrait is a matching portrait of Bunty.

Abby Hello, Emilio. How are you? It's been a while. … No, I haven't received the signed papers yet. When did you send them? … Oh, well, they should get there in a few days … What? … What do you mean, where am I? I'm at home. … Oh, well, I was at the doctor's this morning and I switch my phone off in the surgery. Mum used to

Narrowboat Blues

say it interferes with the equipment on cloud nine or something. So how's your new floozie? ... Oh, I'm sorry to hear that. Well, I'm sure you'll get it sorted out soon.

Chas *(offstage)* Hello, anybody home? *(enters but remains standing at top of steps, i.e. on foredeck, stoops to peep into lounge)*

Abby Chas! *(to phone)* Look, there's someone at the door. I'll call you back.

Chas Can I come in?

Abby But I thought…

Chas What?

Abby I thought you were… they said you… your boat… sank and…

Chas Yes, all gone.

Abby They said… 'Death on the Rochdale Canal'.

Chas I know... Lucy.

Abby I don't understand. What happened?

Chas I was trying to help a kid who'd got hit by a flying windlass and I lost control of the boat. Lucy was trapped in the cabin. Didn't stand a chance.

Abby Oh, my god. But you're alive!

Chas Last time I checked.

They embrace.

Chas I only just heard about Tom and Bunty. I'm so sorry. I'm afraid I've been out of it for a bit. It's taken a while for

Narrowboat Blues

	me to get myself straight. The boat's a write-off, I'm afraid.
Abby	But you're here now… and there's something I have to tell you.
Chas	And there's something I have to say to you.
Abby	OK. You first.
Chas	Well, I've done a lot of thinking and I was coming back for you when the accident happened. And now your parents are gone, too. It's just us now. I guess it's the way of the waterways. People come and go, but the cut don't care. Life goes on.
Abby	So sad about Lucy.
Chas	I know.
Abby	But you know what you were saying about 'life goes on'…

Abby takes his hand and places it over her belly.

The spirits of Tom and Bunty emerge from the wings. The cast sing an upbeat version of Narrowboat Blues. Audience is invited to join in.

>*Refrain:*
>
>I got the blues. I got the blues.
>I got the lonesome narrowboat blues.
>I got the blues. I got the blues.
>I got the lonesome *[or: local place name]* narrowboat blues.
>
>I moved on board when I <u>found</u> my gal.
>Now I put my faith in the old *[or: local name]* canal.

Narrowboat Blues

Refrain

Time is passing by and I'm losing my hair.
People come and go but the cut don't care.

Refrain

Curtain.

Appendix 1   Music

Words and music are the author's own work, but the version below is not necessarily binding on the production. The play provides ample scope for improvisation and variation.

Narrowboat Blues

Narrowboat Blues

Appendix 2   Set design

Whilst the unusual setting may at first appear challenging, there is no real difference between the inside of a narrowboat and a small flat or bedsit, except that the main items of furniture are set out in a line against a (real or imagined) wall with the distance to the fourth wall representing a space of no more than seven feet.

In practice, this means that the interior of the boat can be represented by a few simple items.

To save space and reduce props, either the kitchen unit or the solid fuel stove could be dispensed with. To provide additional seating, the settee bunk could be a corner unit, but any other type of seating can also be used.

If desired, a few traditional narrowboat items could be placed on a shelf or painted on a flat. Any décor is acceptable, but roses & castles, polished brass, chintzy lace, and Laura Ashley would be ideal. A small TV could be included, typically positioned in a corner.

In a full set, the bedroom (or an additional bunk) could be visible stage left. A more elaborate version might include curtained boat windows, a railway-carriage style dinette and a bedroom, separated by partitions where necessary.

Appendix 3   Properties list

Items are listed according to the scene in which they first appear.

Scene 1
Mobile phone (Bunty)
Laptop
Bluetooth speaker
Kettle
Bottle of Aquasol
Mugs and tea-making necessities
Shopping bag
Bunty's coat

Scene 3
Luggage – small suitcase, travel rucksack or similar
Shopping bags (full)
Large pack of incontinence pads
Toilet rolls
Bulk pack of beer (heavy)

Scene 4
Drinks
Cake
Candles
Crockery
Cake forks
Guitar
Windlass (gift wrapped)

Scene 5
Laundry basket
Hammer

Scene 6
Portrait of Tom
Bottle of brandy and glasses

Scene 7
Portrait of Bunty
Mobile phone (Abby)

Appendix 4   Sound effects

Scene 1
Whistling kettle (optional)

Scene 2
Voice of Alexa (unless spoken live)

Scene 3
Sound of vacuum flush toilet (optional)
Sound of hammering (can be performed live)

Scenes 6
Voice of Alexa (unless spoken live)

Scene 7
Instrumental backing (optional)

www.ingramcontent.com/pod-product-compliance
Lightning Source LLC
Chambersburg PA
CBHW061517040426
42450CB00008B/1671